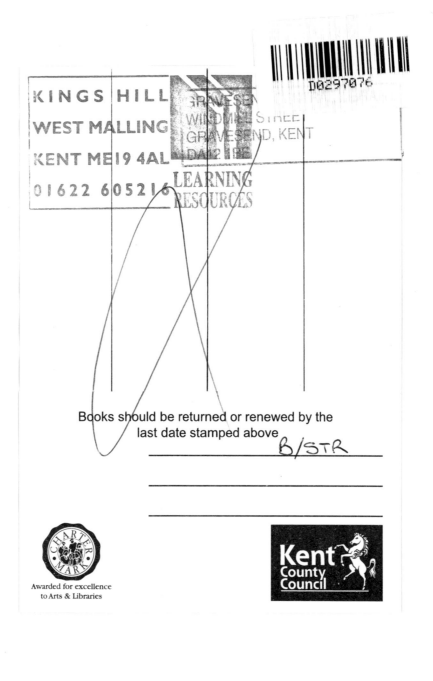

The Life of
Levi Strauss

Tiffany Peterson

H www.heinemann/library.co.uk
Visit our website to find out more information about Heinemann Library books.

To order:
☎ Phone 44 (0) 1865 888066
📄 Send a fax to 44 (0) 1865 314091
💻 Visit the Heinemann Library Bookshop at www.heinemann/library.co.uk to browse our catalogue and order online.

First published in Great Britain by Heinemann Library,
Halley Court, Jordan Hill, Oxford OX2 8EJ,
part of Harcourt Education.
Heinemann is a registered trademark of Harcourt Education Ltd.

Editorial: Angela McHaney Brown, Kathy Peltan
Design: Herman Adler Design
Maps: Mapping Specialists
Picture Research: Dawn Friedman
Production: Edward Moore

Originated by QueNet Media™
Printed and bound by Lake Book Manufacturing, Inc., USA

ISBN 0 431 18070 9
07 06 05 04 03
10 9 8 7 6 5 4 3 2 1

British Library Cataloguing in Publication Data

Peterson, Tiffany
    The Life of Levi Strauss
    338.7'6871'092

A full catalogue record for this book is available from the British Library.

Acknowledgements
The author and publishers are grateful to the following for permission to reproduce copyright material:
p. 4 Ariel Skelley/Corbis; pp. 5, 20 AP Wide World Photos; p. 6 Frank Boxler/AP Wide World Photos; pp. 7, 11 Bettmann/Corbis; p. 8 North Wind Picture Archive; pp. 9, 12, 15, 21 The Granger Collection, New York; p. 10 Jacqui Hurst/Corbis; p. 14 Hulton Archive/Getty Images; pp. 16, 17, 18 The Advertising Archive; p. 19 WarlingStudio/Heinemann Library; pp. 22, 25 Roger Ressmeyer/Corbis; p. 23 Thomas Houseworth Photo/Courtesy San Francisco History Center/neg. #8033; p. 24 Theophilus d'Estrella/The California School for the Deaf; p. 26 Gail Mooney/Corbis; p. 27 Morton Beebe/Corbis; p. 28 Robert Holmes/Corbis; p. 29 Levi Strauss & Company

Cover photographs by SuperStock, Brian Warling/Heinemann Library.

Special thanks to Michelle Rimsa for her comments in the preparation of this book.

Disclaimer
All the Internet addresses (URLs) given in this book were valid at the time of going to press. However, due to the dynamic nature of the Internet, some addresses may have changed, or sites may have changed or ceased to exist since publication. While the author and Publishers regret any inconvenience this may cause readers, no responsibility for any such changes can be accepted by either the author or the Publishers.

Contents

Any words in bold, **like this**, are explained in the Glossary

Everyone wears blue jeans

Most people have a pair of jeans. Many people wear blue jeans: adults, children, even babies. Jeans are popular with people all over the world.

Jeans are worn all over the world.

Jeans were first made for people who had tough and dirty jobs. They needed trousers that would not rip or fall apart. The man who made them was called Levi Strauss.

Levi Strauss started making jeans in 1873.

The early years

This house in Buttenheim, Germany, is where the Strauss family lived.

Levi Strauss was born on 26 February 1829 in Buttenheim, Germany. His first name then was Loeb. Loeb's father sold household items as a **pedlar**, walking through the town.

In 1845, when Loeb was sixteen, his father died. Two years later, Loeb moved with his mother and sisters to the USA.

Loeb's older brothers, Jonas and Louis, already lived in the city of New York, USA.

A new home and a new name

The Strauss family travelled by ship to New York City. The trip took more than a month. Because they were poor, they had to stay in a big, crowded room with no windows.

The Strauss family travelled to the USA in a ship like this one.

This picture from the time shows the busy New York port area with many travellers arriving.

When his family arrived in the USA, Loeb was given a more common name, Levi. He loved his new country and quickly learned to speak English.

Brothers in business

Levi's brothers sold household goods in New York, as their father had done in Germany. They taught Levi the business. Levi worked selling items from a bag he carried on his back.

Levi sold what were known as **dry goods**, such as needles, thread and pots.

Levi knew he would sell more goods if he left New York City. It was hard work, but he enjoyed travelling. He went to the state of Kentucky, about 900 kilometres (560 miles) south-west of New York.

Many people sold things in the streets, shops and markets of New York City.

The California gold rush

While he was in Kentucky, Levi heard stories about the California **gold rush**. Thousands of people were making the long journey to the western state of California. They wanted to find gold.

Levi heard stories about the many people finding gold in California.

Levi went back to New York City, where his brothers now had a shop. He did not stay long. He packed up supplies from Jonas and Louis's shop and left on a ship for California.

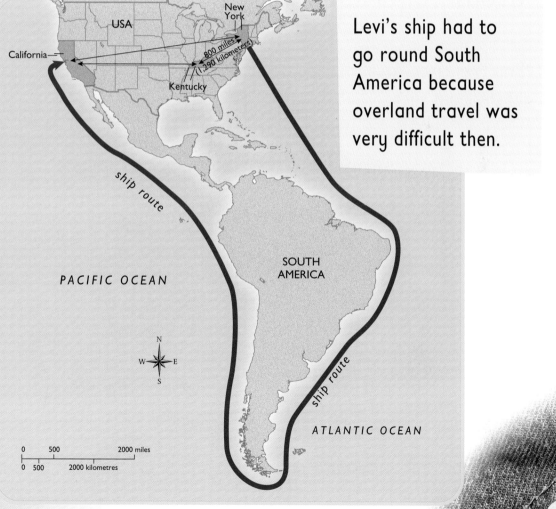

Levi's ship had to go round South America because overland travel was very difficult then.

Moving west

Levi arrived in San Francisco, California in March 1853. His sister Fanny and her husband moved there, too. Together, they started a business selling the household goods from New York.

San Francisco grew quickly because of the gold rush.

Many newly arrived gold miners lived in tents.

People now say that one of the things Levi brought to California was **canvas**. He thought gold miners would need to buy canvas to make tents to live in.

Waist-high overalls

Instead of tents, the men said they needed strong trousers. Levi had an idea. He asked a **tailor** to make some trousers from his thick **canvas** material.

Levi's first trousers were made from beige canvas.

The canvas trousers were strong. The men liked them because they did not tear easily. Levi soon became famous all over California. His trousers were called Levi Strauss **waist-high overalls.**

The Levi Strauss waist-high overalls became very popular.

Better trousers

A **tailor** named Jacob Davis used metal **rivets** to make trouser pockets stronger. They were so popular, he could not make them fast enough. Levi decided to use Jacob's rivets on his **canvas** trousers.

Levi and Jacob got a **patent** in 1873 so that only Levi Strauss & Company could make trousers with rivets.

Levi thought of a **logo** for his trousers. It was a picture of two horses trying to pull apart a pair of his trousers. The picture was burned on to small pieces of leather and stitched on to the back of the trousers.

The Levi's logo still shows the same picture today.

A growing business

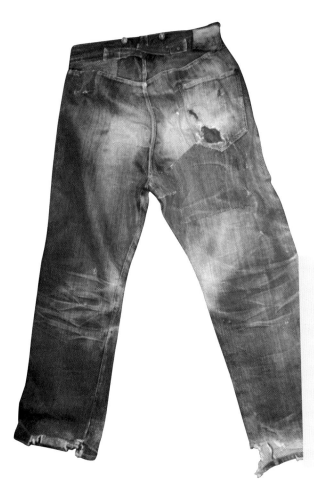

The Levi Strauss Museum in San Francisco has pairs of Levi's jeans that are over 100 years old!

Levi worked hard to make his trousers even better. Instead of beige **canvas**, he started making trousers from blue **denim**. His business grew.

Levi was becoming a rich and important man. He employed more people. He opened bigger **factories**. Unlike many bosses, Levi spent time with his workers.

Levi Strauss & Company had its own office building in San Francisco.

Later life

Levi never got married or had any children. He employed his nephews to help run his company. He taught them everything about the business.

In a **factory**, many pairs of jeans can be made at the same time.

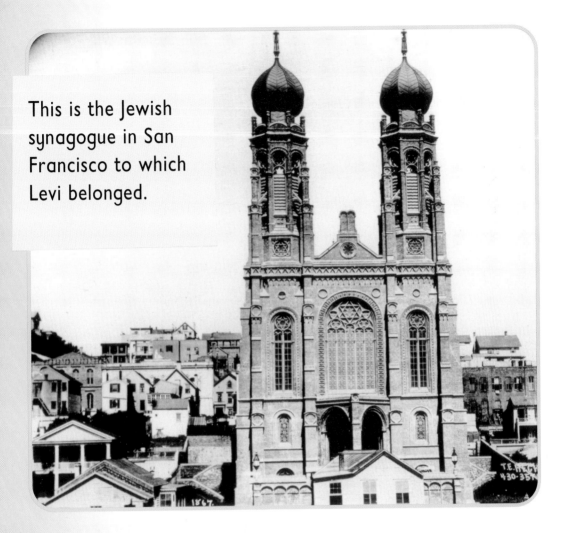

This is the Jewish synagogue in San Francisco to which Levi belonged.

Levi decided he wanted to use his money to help people. Each year he gave money to his **synagogue**. The money paid for gold medals that were given to the best students.

The company goes on

In 1902, Levi Strauss became ill. He died on 26 September. Even after his death, Levi Strauss helped others. He left money to children's homes and for elderly people.

Levi also gave money to schools, including the California School for the Deaf, shown here.

Levi's nephews made sure his company did well. They began making other clothes, as well as jeans. Levi's now makes trousers, shirts and baby clothes.

Levi's jeans are still popular today.

The company today

Shops that sell only Levi's products are found all over the world.

Today, Levi Strauss & Company is still run by members of Levi's family. Levi's jeans and other clothes are sold and worn all over the world.

Levi's jeans can be bought in more than 160 countries. The company has more than 12,000 workers worldwide.

Levi Plaza in San Francisco is the location of the main office of the company in the USA.

Helping people

The name Levi Strauss lives on. Levi is best known today for making blue **denim** jeans. But he is also remembered for giving money to help others.

In 1897, Levi gave money for 28 yearly **scholarships** at the University of California, USA.

In 1952, Levi Strauss & Company created the Levi Strauss Foundation. A foundation is a group that helps others. The Levi Strauss Foundation gives money to help children all over the world go to school.

The Foundation also supports community art projects and education programmes.

Fact file

- Levi Strauss's childhood home in Germany is now a museum.

- Levi Strauss & Company still owns one of Levi's first factories in San Francisco.

- The fabric Levi used to make jeans was first called *serge de Nîmes*. That meant the fabric was from Nîmes in France. The name was later shortened to **denim**.

- '501' was the number given to the denim used for the first Levi's jeans.

- In 1906, an earthquake destroyed most of the Levi Strauss & Company offices and factories. New buildings were soon built.

Timeline

26 February 1829	Loeb Strauss is born in Buttenheim, Germany
1847	Loeb, his mother and his sisters move to the USA Loeb's name becomes Levi
1848	Levi moves to Kentucky
1853	Levi moves to California
1854	Levi opens his first shop in San Francisco
1866	Levi Strauss & Company moves into its first offices and **factory**
1873	Levi Strauss and Jacob Davis get a **patent** for **rivets** and begin adding them to Levi's trousers
26 September 1902	Levi dies at the age of 73

Glossary

canvas strong, thick fabric used to make tents

denim strong, cotton fabric that is usually blue

dry goods household items, such as cloth, thread and needles

factory place where things are made

gold rush when many people move to an area to find gold

logo picture that stands for a product

patent legal paper given to a person that says he or she is the only person allowed to make a certain invention unless he or she gives permission to someone else

pedlar someone who travels around selling the goods they carry with them

rivet small metal stud used to strengthen pocket corners

scholarship money given to a student to help pay for education

synagogue building used by Jewish people for worship and for classes about religion

tailor person who makes clothes

waist-high overalls original name for jeans; any loose-fitting trousers

More books to read

Dead Famous: Inventors and Their Bright Ideas, Mike Goldsmith, (Hippo, 2002)

Materials: Cotton, Chris Oxlade, (Heinemann Library, 2001)

Index